A VISIT TO

Japan

REVISED AND UPDATED

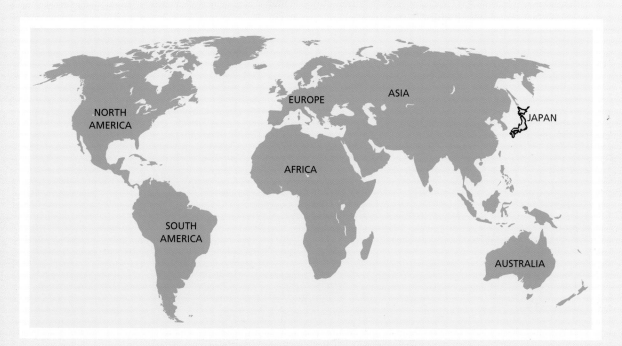

Peter and Connie Roop

Heinemann Library
Chicago, Illinois

Designed by Heinemann Library
Printed and bound in the United States of America, North Mankato, Minnesota.

16 15 14
10 9 8 7 6

Library of Congress Cataloging-in-Publication Data
Roop, Peter.
        Japan / Peter & Connie Roop.
p.   cm. – (Visit to)
Includes Index.
Summary: Introduces the country of Japan, including the land,
landmarks, homes, food, clothes, work, transportation, language,
school, sports, celebrations, and the arts.
ISBN 978-1-4329-1271-0 (lib.bdg.) ISBN 978-1-4329-1290-1 (pbk.)
1.   Japan—Pictorial works—juvenile literature. [1. Japan.]
I. Roop, Connie. II. Series: Roop, Peter. Visit to.
DS806.R56   1998   98-12448
952—dc21
012014   007944RP

Acknowledgements
The publishers would like to thank the following for permission to reproduce photographs: © Getty
Images p. **24** (Koichi Kamoshida); © B. Glinn-Magnum p. **20**; © Colorific! p. **28** (de Marcillac); © Corbis
p. **18** (Jose Fuste Raga); © Getty Images p. **13** (Absodels); © Hutchison Library pp. **5** (J. Burbank), **10** (M.
Harvey), **11** (M. Harvey), **22** (J. Burbank), **23** (R. Francis), **29** (J. Burbank); © Images Color Library pp. **8**, **14**,
15, **21**; © J. Allan Cash Ltd pp. **9**, **12**, **16**; © JNTO p. **26**; © Panos Pictures pp. **6** (J. Holmes), **7** (J. Holmes);
© Photolibrary p. **25** (Japan Travel Bureau); © Reuters p. **19** (Kim Kyung Hoon); © Trip p. **27** (C. McCooey).

Cover photograph reproduced with permission of © Photolibrary (Japan Tourist Board).

Our thanks to Nick Lapthorn for his comments in the preparation of this book.

Every effort has been made to contact copyright holders of any material reproduced in this book. Any
omissions will be rectified in subsequent printings if notice is given to the publishers.

Contents

Any words appearing in bold, **like this**, are explained in the Glossary.

Japan

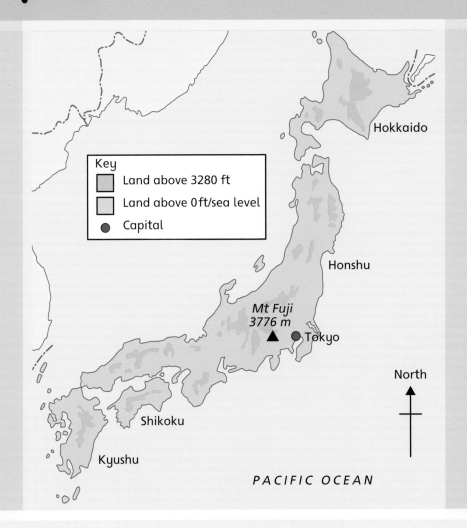

Key
- Land above 3280 ft
- Land above 0 ft/sea level
- ● Capital

Hokkaido

Honshu

Mt Fuji
3776 m
▲ ● Tokyo

North

Shikoku

Kyushu

PACIFIC OCEAN

Japan is an island country in Asia.
The Japanese call their country Nippon,
which means "Land of the Rising Sun."

There are 4,000 islands in Japan. Most people live on the four biggest islands. They are Hokkaido, Honshu, Shikoku, and Kyushu.

Land

Japan has many mountains and **volcanoes**. Some of the volcanoes **erupt**. Also, Japan has about 1,500 **earthquakes** each year.

Japan stretches out for a long way. The north islands can have snow while the south islands are still warm. All of the islands have stormy winds called typhoons.

Many of the islands in Japan are quite small.

Landmarks

Mount Fuji is Japan's most famous mountain. It is a **volcano**. It has not **erupted** for hundreds of years.

Tokyo is the **capital**. It is Japan's largest city. One person out of every ten Japanese people lives in Tokyo.

Homes

Most people live in small apartments in crowded cities. Most of the cities are on the lowlands near the coast.

In the country, there are homes made of wood. They are only one or two stories high. Japanese people always take their shoes off when they enter a home.

Food

The Japanese enjoy making their food look attractive. They eat small portions of many different types of food but noodles are a favorite fast food.

At home, many Japanese people sit on the floor and eat from low wooden tables. They use **chopsticks** for all their food. Rice and hot tea are served at every meal.

Clothes

Farmers in the country wear **traditional** work clothes, such as baggy trousers and straw hats. Most Japanese people in the cities wear modern clothes.

Japanese people wear kimonos on special days.

Kimonos are long silk robes which are tied with a large sash. There is a different kimono for each season. The light, summer kimonos are called *yukata*.

Work

Only a few Japanese are farmers but they grow most of Japan's food. They grow rice, wheat, soybeans, tea, fruit, and vegetables. They also keep pigs and chickens.

Japan's fishermen are very successful.
They catch more fish than almost anyone
else in the world. Most people in Japan
work in offices or factories.

Transportation

The bullet train is the fastest way to travel on land. There is a rail link between two of the islands through the world's longest tunnel.

The bullet train travels at a speed of 170 miles (270 kilometers) per hour.

So many people travel to work by train or **subway** that passengers are pushed onto them by station workers. Airports and highways link all the main cities.

Language

When Japanese people greet each other, they bow to show **respect**. They speak very politely to each other.

It takes a long time to learn to read and write Japanese. There are 1,850 **characters** which are written in columns from right to left.

School

Children go to school from the age of 6 to 15. They learn lots of different subjects. All Japanese children learn English. They also practise **earthquake drills**.

Most primary school children do not wear a uniform.

Most school children study very hard. Each night they do hours of homework and extra lessons. They work hard to get into a good college.

Free Time

Sumo wrestling is Japan's national sport. Each wrestler has to throw the other one out of the ring. Millions of Japanese also enjoy baseball.

Many Japanese regularly visit parks and gardens. A favorite time to go is in the spring when the cherry trees are in blossom.

This park is in a new city called Ina.

Celebrations

Japan has many festivals but New Year's is the biggest. People eat special food and send each other New Year's cards.

The kites on Children's Day are in the shape of a fish called carp.

Children's Day is a holiday on May 5. People fly kites or **streamers** for the children in the family.

The Arts

There are many **traditional crafts** in Japan, such as ink painting, flower arranging, and making beautiful pottery. Origami is the art of making models by folding paper.

Noh theater has been performed for around 700 years.

Noh is a form of Japanese theater. Actors wear masks to perform **ancient** stories. Musicians are also on stage and in costume, to **accompany** the actors.

Fact File

Name Japan is the full name of the country.

Capital The **capital** of Japan is Tokyo.

Language Most Japanese speak and write Japanese, but some can also speak Korean and English.

Population There are about 127 million people living in Japan.

Money Japanese money is called the yen.

Religions Most Japanese believe in Buddhism and Shintoism. There are also some Christians.

Products Japan produces lots of rice, fish, steel, cameras, televisions, radios, ships, cars, chemicals, and toys.

Words you can learn

ichi (ee-tchee)	one
ni (nee)	two
sahn (san)	three
konnichi wa (kon-nee-tchee-wa)	hello
sayonara (sah-yoh-nah-rah)	goodbye
arigato (aree-gah-toh)	thank you
hai (hi)	yes
iie (ee-eh)	no

Glossary

accompany play an instrument while someone else sings or speaks

ancient from a long time ago

capital city where the government is based

character symbol or letter in a writing system

chopsticks a pair of sticks held in one hand to lift food to the mouth

craft skill in making things

drill a safety routine where people practice what to do when there is a danger, like a fire or an earthquake

earthquake violent shaking of the ground

erupt throw out ash and melted rock

respect to value someone or think highly of them

streamer long piece of paper used as decoration

subway trains that run underground through tunnels

traditional the way things have been done or made for a long time

volcano a mountain or hole in the ground that sometimes throws out ash or melted rock from beneath the Earth's surface

Index